Published by Creative Education
P.O. Box 227, Mankato, Minnesota 56002
Creative Education is an imprint of The Creative Company

Design and production by Blue Design
Printed in the United States of America

Photographs by Getty Images (Brain Bahr, Bruce Bennett Studios, PAUL K. BUCK/AFP, Chris Covatta, Chris Covatta/ Allsport, Jonathan Daniel/Allsport, Diamond Images, Stephen Dunn/Allsport, Otto Greule, Otto Greule Jr/Allsport, Lonnie Major/Allsport, Brad Mangin/MLB Photos, Ronald Martinez, Doug Pensinger, Rich Pilling/MLB Photos, Louis Requena/ MLB Photos, Robert Riger, Don Smith/MLB Photos, Rick Stewart/Allsport, Tony Tomsic/MLB Photos, John Williamson/ MLB Photos)

Library of Congress Cataloging-in-Publication Data

Richardson, Adele, 1966-
The story of the Texas Rangers / by Adele Richardson.
p. cm. — (Baseball: the great American game)
Includes index.
ISBN-13: 978-1-58341-502-3
1. Texas Rangers (Baseball team)—History—Juvenile literature. I. Title. II. Series.

GV875.T4R43 2007
796.357'6409764531—dc22   2006027465

First Edition
9 8 7 6 5 4 3 2 1

Cover: First baseman Mark Teixeira
Page 1: Catcher Ivan Rodriguez
Page 3: Shortstop Michael Young

by Adele Richardson

THE STORY OF THE
Texas Rangers

O n September 26, 1999, the 38,000 fans at The Ballpark at Arlington knew that they were watching the decisive game of the season. The Texas Rangers had already walloped the Oakland Athletics twice that weekend, and their fans hoped that this game would be no different. Texas pulled ahead in the first, putting two runs on the board before the first out. After the Rangers added four more runs in the bottom of the fifth, the crowd began to breathe easier. In the bottom of the sixth, with the bases loaded, Texas first baseman Rafael Palmeiro stepped up to the plate, and Oakland pitcher Doug Jones wound up and delivered. Palmeiro swung—hard—and found the sweet spot, launching a

ball deep for a home run. With one swing, Palmeiro had earned all the runs the Rangers would need that day: for the third time in four years, Texas was going to the playoffs.

An avid baseball fan, President John F.
Kennedy threw out the first pitch of the
Senators' 1961 and 1962 seasons.

HOME ON THE RANGE

Situated between Dallas and Fort Worth, the Texas city of Arlington has come a long way since its humble beginnings in 1876. Under the protection of a mounted police force called the Texas Rangers, settlers began arriving by the hundreds as the century drew to an end. As the Dallas and Fort Worth areas grew in population, the Texas and Pacific Railway also branched out to connect the two cities. Arlington was born on the railway between the two as a market town for nearby farmers. Today, it is a thriving city that is home to nearly 400,000 residents, pro football's Dallas Cowboys, and, since 1972, an American League (AL) baseball franchise.

Like the Texas settlers of long ago, Arlington's baseball team migrated from another part of the country. When the Washington Senators moved from the East Coast to Minnesota in 1960, Major League Baseball awarded the nation's capital another franchise. This one was also named the Senators, and in 1961, President John F. Kennedy threw out the first pitch of its inaugural game.

Team owner Elwood "Pete" Quesada should have picked a different name, though. The D.C. area had a long history of losing with teams named the Senators. This newest incarnation of the 1960s would prove to be no different, posting losing records its first eight seasons, despite the best efforts of players such as brawny left fielder Frank Howard and catcher Paul Casanova.

While the Senators were struggling, other important events were unfolding across the country that would affect the team's future. In 1962, Charley O. Finley, the owner of the Kansas City Athletics baseball team, met with AL team owners in New York. While the owners initially approved his idea of moving his team to the Dallas-Fort Worth area, they ultimately rejected it. But two years later, construction began on the 10,000-seat Turnpike Stadium in Arlington, slated to be the home of a Texas League minor-league team called the Dallas-Fort Worth Spurs.

Back in D.C., legendary Boston Red Sox slugger Ted Williams was hired as manager of the Senators in 1969. Under his guidance, the team posted its first season over .500, going 86–76. Pitcher Dick Bosman turned in an im-

THE LONGEST NIGHT

What did Washington Senators and Chicago White Sox players have in common after a June 12–13 game in 1967? Nearly seven hours of baseball and a lot of explaining to do to their families about just where they had been. When the game started at 8:00 P.M. in D.C. Stadium, no one planned for it to go into extra innings. But at the end of the ninth, the game was tied 4–4. Chicago pulled ahead in the 10th, but a wild pitch by Sox hurler Bob Locker and a sacrifice fly during the Senators' half of the inning tied it back up. The clock kept ticking, and neither team had any success for the next 11 innings. Finally, in the bottom of the 22nd inning, the stalemate ended. An exhausted White Sox pitching staff walked two batters and allowed one single. Then, Senators catcher Paul Casanova singled to left, driving in a run and ending the contest with a 6–5 victory. The game was finally over at 2:43 in the morning. The excessively late-playing game caused the league to set a curfew about long-running games. Since then, no inning has been allowed to start after 1:00 A.M.; the game is simply listed as an official tie.

FRANK HOWARD

THE WIN THAT NEVER WAS

The Washington Senators' final game was played at home on September 30, 1971. The team was moving to Texas the next season and wanted to go out with a win—especially against the rival New York Yankees—and it looked as if that was going to happen at last. Going into the ninth inning, the Senators were leading 7–5. Senators pitcher Joe Grzenda took the mound to toss to New York's Felipe Alou. The pinch hitter swung hard but managed only to dribble a slow roller back to Grzenda, who threw to first for the out. Next up was Yankees center fielder Bobby Murcer. After a few pitches, Murcer duplicated Alou's hit, grounding the ball back to the mound for an easy out. With the win apparently imminent, Washington fans began swarming onto the field of Robert F. Kennedy Stadium. The umpires couldn't clear the mass of spectators no matter how hard they tried. In the end, the swan-song game for the departing Senators ended up being called a draw. While the team neither won nor lost the game, the soon-to-be Rangers left D.C. knowing that they would certainly be missed by the hometown crowd.

[9]

pressive season, ending with an AL-best 2.19 earned run average (ERA), and Howard chalked up 48 home runs. Williams earned the 1969 AL Manager of the Year award for his efforts, and Senators fans began dreaming of bigger things.

Unfortunately, the Senators would have only a small taste of success. They were back under .500 in 1970 and closed 1971 a dismal 63–96. Interest in baseball waned in D.C., not only because they had a losing team, but also because people were more concerned about the Vietnam War. Owner Robert E. Short saw this disinterest as an opportunity to move his franchise to Texas. In 1972, the Senators settled in Arlington with a new name; Short dubbed them the Texas Rangers, in honor of the legendary lawmen of the West.

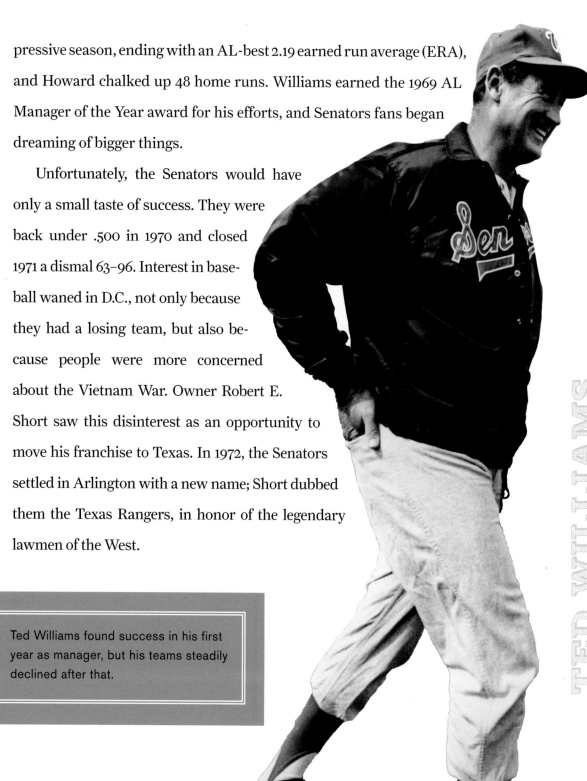

Ted Williams found success in his first year as manager, but his teams steadily declined after that.

TED WILLIAMS

PITCHER · CHARLIE HOUGH

In 1969, Charlie Hough suffered an arm injury and had to learn a different way to pitch. After Los Angeles Dodgers scout Goldie Holt was done with him, Hough had acquired what would soon become his signature pitch: the knuckleball. During his Texas career, Hough averaged 15 wins and 240 innings pitched per season. At the peak of his career in 1983, he hurled three straight shutouts and threw 37 consecutive scoreless innings. Four years later, the 39-year-old became the oldest pitcher in AL history to lead the league in starts (40) and innings pitched (285).

CHARLIE HOUGH
PITCHER

TEXAS
RANGERS

STATS

Rangers seasons: 1980–90

Height: 6-2

Weight: 190

- **2,362 career strikeouts**
- **107 career complete games**
- **3.75 career ERA**
- **13 career shutouts**

THE STRUGGLES CONTINUE

Before the Rangers donned their new red, white, and blue uniforms, Turnpike Stadium had to be expanded. The seating capacity was nearly doubled, and the home grounds were given the new name Arlington Stadium. Ted Williams stayed on as skipper, and Texas fans hoped the changes signaled a fresh start for the franchise.

Unfortunately, the 1972 Rangers posted an embarrassingly bad record of 54–100. Frank Howard, whose fine hitting in 1969 had helped lead the team to its only winning season, was traded in August, and Williams retired at the end of the year. Still, there were some bright spots in 1972. Outfielder Ted Ford led the team in home runs (14) and doubles (19), and shortstop Toby Harrah was named the Rangers' first All-Star.

In 1973, the Rangers showed modest improvement, but it was the 1974 season that caught fans' attention and generated record attendance levels for the young Texas team. Harrah was still putting up big numbers, but left fielder Jeff Burroughs led the team with 25 long balls and 118 RBI—a performance that earned him the AL Most Valuable Player (MVP) award that year and a trip to the All-Star Game. The Rangers' pitching efforts improved, too. Fergie

CATCHER · IVAN RODRIGUEZ

Known as "I-Rod" by some and "Pudge" by most, Rodriguez was the rare player who seemed to get better with age. After signing with the Rangers in 1991, Pudge's offensive and defensive numbers consistently rose. His skill behind the plate in blocking balls thrown in the dirt was complemented by his powerful right arm, which routinely gunned down the best base stealers in the majors. Rodriguez was the first AL catcher to post a .300 or higher batting average five seasons in a row, and at age 29, he became the youngest backstop ever to reach the 1,000 career hits mark.

STATS

Rangers seasons: 1991–2002

Height: 5-9

Weight: 205

- **12-time Gold Glove winner**
- **13-time All-Star**
- **2,354 career hits**
- **.304 career BA**

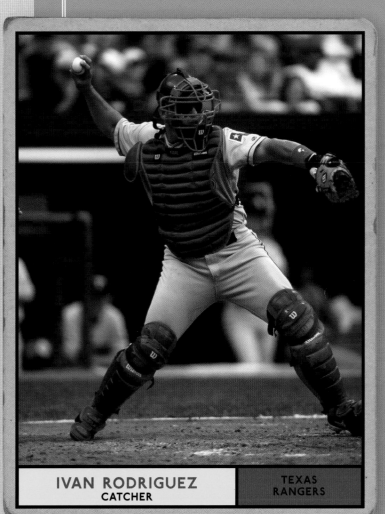

IVAN RODRIGUEZ
CATCHER

TEXAS
RANGERS

FIRST BASEMAN · RAFAEL PALMEIRO

When Rafael Palmeiro started his major-league career in 1986, he was considered strictly a singles hitter. Four years later, he got into the swing of things—literally. During his career, "Raffy" strung together nine consecutive seasons of 38 or more home runs and 100 or more RBI. The four-time All-Star could also play some defense, winning the 1999 Gold Glove even though he played only 28 games at first that year (he was used as a designated hitter for the rest). The Cuban-born Palmeiro was one of only four players ever to attain 500 career home runs and 3,000 career hits.

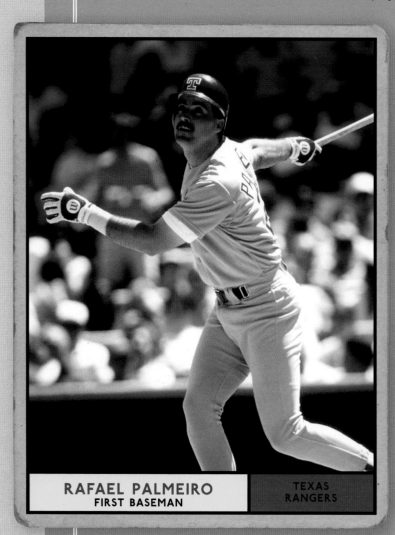

RAFAEL PALMEIRO
FIRST BASEMAN

TEXAS
RANGERS

STATS

Rangers seasons: 1989–93, 1999–2003

Height: 6-0

Weight: 215

- **3-time Gold Glove winner**
- **12 career grand slams**
- **3,020 career hits**
- **569 career HR**

Jenkins led the league with 25 wins and nearly won the Cy Young Award as the best pitcher in the league. When later asked about his dominating season, Jenkins replied: "I didn't consider pitching to be work—I was having fun getting most hitters out."

For the next few years, the Rangers' lineup featured solid veterans and some young, impressive players who would soon find their grooves. First baseman Mike Hargrove was named AL Rookie of the Year in 1974 after posting a career-high .323 average. Nicknamed "The Human Rain Delay" for his tendency to linger at the plate before a pitch to analyze every possible outcome, Hargrove was a source of stability for the Rangers and, in 1975, was named an All-Star. Future Hall of Fame pitcher Gaylord Perry joined the Texas crew that year, adding depth to the Rangers' rotation. Despite the never-ending changes to their roster, the Rangers hung

FERGIE JENKINS

SECOND BASEMAN · MARK McLEMORE

In 1986, Mark McLemore made his major-league debut with the California Angels at the tender age of 21, but it wasn't until the 1990s that he really made a name for himself. McLemore became known as a versatile player whose terrific all-around game helped carry his team to the postseason seven times during his career. Even though injuries kept the second-sacker sidelined on and off for much of his career, preventing him from being an everyday player, coaches always looked to McLemore when they needed someone to come through with a pinch hit or reliable defense.

MARK McLEMORE
SECOND BASEMAN

TEXAS
RANGERS

STATS

Rangers seasons: 1995–99

Height: 5-11

Weight: 207

- **1,602 career hits**

- **943 career runs scored**

- **255 career doubles**

- **.259 career BA**

AL OLIVER

below second place in the AL West throughout the '70s. Management made more moves in 1978, trading veteran Toby Harrah to the Cleveland Indians for third baseman Buddy Bell, and hiring Pat Corrales as the latest in an already long line of skippers.

A new decade brought a new team owner, Texas oil magnate Eddie Chiles, in 1980. Bell batted a career-high .329 that year, and knuckleball ace Charlie Hough came to "the Gunslingers" in July from the Los Angeles Dodgers and soon became a fan favorite. Outfielder Al Oliver, who would spend four years in Texas without ever letting his bat cool below .309, led the team with 117 RBI in 1980. But the Rangers again finished deep in the standings, more than 20 games out of first place.

For the next six years, the Rangers suffered a steady downhill slide. Corrales left in 1981, and three more skippers tried unsuccessfully to guide

EXTRA-INNING BLOWOUT

Scoring 12 runs in a game does not happen every day in the big leagues. And it's much more rare to score 12 runs in one inning. And to score 12 runs in one extra inning? That's practically unheard-of. Yet that's exactly what the Rangers did against the Oakland A's on July 3, 1983. Texas took a 2–0 lead in the fourth inning and held it until the A's tied up the game in the ninth. The teams swung and missed for five more innings until the 15th, when Rangers shortstop Russell Dent was walked in the top half of the inning. After a single and an intentional walk, the bases were loaded. Then Texas outfielder Bob Jones doubled, driving in two runs. The shaken Oakland pitcher's next throw sailed wild, scoring another Rangers run and moving a player to third. A new pitcher came in, but the Rangers were on a roll. Before the inning was out, the team had sent 16 batters to the plate. Texas won the game 16–4, setting a major-league record for runs scored in one extra inning.

THIRD BASEMAN · DEAN PALMER

The same player who led the AL in strikeouts in 1992 (with 154) was, by 1998, an AL All-Star. In Dean Palmer's rookie year, he played all over the field for the Rangers, but by 1992, his position at third had solidified, and he became known as one of the AL's most consistent third-sackers. Palmer's best offensive years were in 1998 and 1999, when he was awarded the Silver Slugger award as the best-hitting third baseman in the league. Always willing to do whatever it took to get on base, he racked up 502 walks over the course of his career.

DEAN PALMER
THIRD BASEMAN

TEXAS
RANGERS

STATS

Rangers seasons: 1989, 1991–97

Height: 6-1

Weight: 210

- **1,229 career hits**
- **849 career RBI**
- **2-time Silver Slugger award winner**
- **231 career doubles**

GAYLORD PERRY

the team above .500. When manager Bobby Valentine came on board in 1985, the Rangers assembled a 62–99 mark. After Bell was traded to the Cincinnati Reds in July 1985, ending the Texas tenure of the six-time Gold Glove winner, Rangers management was convinced it was time for a change. It kept Valentine as manager but started looking for new talent.

BOBBY WITT – With a blistering fastball and a reputation as a wild thrower, Witt alternately sparkled and struggled early in his big-league career. In 1986 and 1987, he led all AL pitchers in both strikeouts and walks per nine innings pitched.

GREAT EXPECTATIONS

Bobby Valentine's roster on opening day of 1986 included 10 rookies, but he did have a few veterans on whom he could count. Shortstop Scott Fletcher, a five-year veteran, led the team by batting a solid .300. On the pitching front, Hough posted yet another double-digit win total and mentored rookie hurler Bobby Witt and hard-throwing closer Mitch Williams. Impressively, the Rangers closed 1986 in second place in the AL Western Division, only five games behind the California Angels.

The Rangers finished the next two seasons under .500, but after some additional player moves, the franchise put together its most formidable roster yet. Fans flocked to Arlington Stadium in 1989, breaking the two million mark for the first time in club history. And they had good reason to show up. Two rookies, third baseman Dean Palmer and right fielder Juan Gonzalez, showed lots of promise—Palmer for his flexibility in playing multiple positions in the field, and Gonzalez for his ability to swat home runs. Power hitter Rafael Palmeiro manned first base, and newly signed strikeout king Nolan Ryan commanded the mound. "My job is to give my team a chance to win," Ryan said. And he delivered. The "Ryan Express" closed the

1989 season with 16 wins, earning his 5,000th career strikeout along the way. Together, this mix of power and pitching carried the team to a 83–79 finish.

More standouts emerged during the Rangers' 1990 season. Outfielder Ruben Sierra, who had posted a league-leading 119 RBI in 1989, notched 96 more, and Palmeiro led the team in batting with a .319 average. Ryan's win total dropped to 13, but second-year pitcher Kenny Rogers produced his first 10-win season. Despite some fine individual play, the team finished third in the AL West, 20 games behind the first-place Oakland A's.

Attendance records were broken again in Arlington Stadium in 1991. Fans clearly saw the potential of their team, but the Rangers again failed to find consistency. The main highlight that year came from the mound, as Ryan hurled his seventh career no-hitter at the age of 44 against the Toronto Blue Jays. Still, no Rangers hurler could manage more than 13 wins. At the plate, the Rangers were dangerous, with Palmeiro, Sierra, and second baseman Julio Franco all batting .307 or greater. Behind the plate, rookie catcher Ivan "Pudge" Rodriguez thrilled fans with his bullet-like throws to second to stop would-be base stealers. The team ended with its third straight winning season but remained far out of the playoff picture.

Desperate for more than just a winning season, Rangers management

UAN GONZALEZ

Juan Gonzalez's booming bat earned him five Silver Slugger awards during his outstanding Rangers career.

NOLAN RYAN

An impossibly strong right arm let
Nolan Ryan throw 100-mile-per-hour
heat and play 27 big-league seasons.

SHORTSTOP · TOBY HARRAH

Despite posting a lackluster .230 batting average in his first major-league season, Toby Harrah became a force to be reckoned with, both at the plate and in the field. During the mid-1970s, Harrah found his groove, putting together five 20-home-run seasons and posting high numbers of walks and runs. In 1977, Harrah and Rangers second baseman Bump Wills accomplished something done only once before in big-league history, hitting back-to-back inside-the-park home runs. The versatile Harrah was just as comfortable playing third base as he was shortstop.

STATS

Rangers seasons: 1969, 1971 (Washington Senators), 1972–78, 1985–86

Height: 6-0

Weight: 180

- **4-time All-Star**

- **1,954 career hits**

- **918 career RBI**

- **238 career stolen bases**

TOBY HARRAH
SHORTSTOP

TEXAS RANGERS

fired Valentine in the middle of the 1992 season. Fan favorite Toby Harrah was brought in to finish out the year at the helm but was himself replaced before opening day of 1993. Palmeiro was traded to the Baltimore Orioles at the end of that season, and Ryan retired. But even with such losses, positive change seemed to be in the air after Texas finished 1993 in second place in the AL West.

The Rangers moved into a new home, The Ballpark at Arlington, in 1994 and seemed poised to make a run for the postseason. Rogers threw the first perfect game in Rangers history against the California Angels, and rookie center fielder Rusty Greer awed fans and opponents alike with his diving plays in the outfield, sliding for brilliant catches or crashing into outfield walls on an almost nightly basis. The Rangers hung close to first place for most of the year. But when a players' strike cut the season short in August, their hopes for the postseason were cut along with it. Technically, the 1994 Rangers finished in first place in the AL West, but since no awards were handed out, the victory was a hollow one.

HARD WORK PAYS OFF

ith the players' strike over, fans and players were ready for a new beginning in 1995. The Rangers had arguably more talent than ever before. Rodriguez's batting average increased to .303 that 1995 season, while Palmer led the team with a .336 average. Outfielder Mickey Tettleton connected for 32 dingers, and southpaw Kenny Rogers led the pitching rotation again with 17 wins. Yet turning strong individual performances into team success remained a struggle. The franchise had brought in Johnny Oates in hopes he could carry the team upward with his quiet, methodical ways, but the Rangers still finished four and a half games behind the division-champion Seattle Mariners.

With Will "The Thrill" Clark manning first, Pudge still gunning down base runners from behind the plate, and the pitching staff winning a franchise-record 90 games, it seemed as if 1996 would finally be the Rangers' year. Under Oates's guidance, the team pulled together and stayed near first. As September waned, Palmer and Gonzalez kept hitting long balls, and the Rangers pulled away from the competition, at long last clinching the AL West title with a 90–72 record. Although they lost to the New York Yankees in three postseason games, the team set new standards for success. Longtime

CANCELLED PLANS

The 1994 season was supposed to be a great one for the Rangers. Construction was finally completed on the new $191-million The Ballpark at Arlington, and an exhibition game was scheduled with the New York Mets for April 1. But by the end of the game, won by New York 10–7, it was clear that it would take more than a new stadium to turn the Rangers into winners. Three days later, opening day in Yankee Stadium brought another loss for the Texas team. The club returned to Texas and prepared for its first regular-season game at home against the Milwaukee Brewers, but staying true to form, the Rangers lost again. Even though the season started off dismally, the Rangers did manage their share of wins; by August 12, their record stood at 52–62, and Texas was in first place in the AL West. But that day, a players' strike began that would last 232 days and lead to the cancellation of 920 major-league games. When the big-league brass eventually called the season a bust, the Rangers' first chance at a division title was denied, along with their plans for postseason play.

KENNY ROGERS

Crafty hurler Kenny Rogers spent
three different stints with the Rangers,
spanning the 1989 to 2005 seasons.

LEFT FIELDER · FRANK HOWARD

Frank Howard's teammates dubbed him "The Capital Punisher" with good reason. In May 1968 (while the team was still the Washington Senators), The Punisher went on a slugging rampage that set a major-league record. In six consecutive games, the heavy-handed Howard bashed 10 home runs in 20 at bats. He was no slouch in the field, either. Besides holding down left field, Howard spent a significant amount of time at first base and in right field. The Punisher's bat remained powerful for many seasons, and toward the end of his career, he played mainly as a designated hitter.

STATS

Rangers seasons: 1965–71 (Washington Senators), 1972

Height: 6-7

Weight: 255

- **4-time All-Star**
- **1,774 career hits**
- **1,119 career RBI**
- **382 career HR**

FRANK HOWARD
LEFT FIELDER

TEXAS
RANGERS

star Juan Gonzalez's 47 homers earned him AL MVP honors, while Oates's leadership brought him the AL Manager of the Year award.

Compared with the thrills of the previous season, 1997 was quiet in Texas. The franchise brought in veteran closer John Wetteland from the Yankees, and Bobby Witt made history on June 30 by becoming the first Rangers pitcher ever to crack a homer. But the team's numbers fell all across the board, and Texas slumped back to third place.

Knowing that a team can do something and making it happen are two different things. Still, Oates knew that his players had it in them to make it to the postseason again. In 1998, the Rangers' reliable hitters stayed reliable, and the pitching staff bounced back to form. That season and the next, Texas brought home the AL West crown. Both years, the team's bats were more than hot— they were on fire. Palmeiro's return from Baltimore in 1999 added 47 homers to the Rangers' offense. "He could hit .320 or 45 homers," said Texas picher Kenny Rogers. "He's chosen the latter right now. He wants 45 homers a year and nobody can complain. He does it year in and year out." Rodriguez's numbers were also on the rise, and his career-high 35 home runs and 113 RBI earned him the 1999 AL MVP award.

Gonzalez, meanwhile, remained an offensive powerhouse. In 9 seasons with the Rangers, he averaged 37 homers a year and earned 2 AL MVP awards (1996 and 1998). "He is unbelievably strong," Palmeiro said of the outfielder.

"And yet has such quick hands. Even when he gets fooled [by a pitch], he can recover and then just snap his wrists—and the ball goes 450 feet."

Wetteland was also a key factor in the team's first-place finishes in 1998 and 1999. During his four years in Texas, he would average 38 saves a season. But despite their talent and accolades, the Rangers still came up short of the World Series in the postseason. In both 1998 and 1999, the Yankees mercilessly swept the Rangers from the playoffs in three straight games.

JOHN WETTELAND – Suiting up for four different teams, Wetteland earned more saves (295) than any other pitcher in the 1990s. He ended the decade in fine style, nailing down a Rangers-record 43 saves in 1999 and earning a place on the AL All-Star team.

A NEW-CENTURY TEAM

he Rangers had every intention of riding the adrenaline from the year before into the 2000 season. But before they could begin, Gonzalez left town and took his booming bat with him. The rest of the lineup cooled off as well, and the 2000 Rangers sank to fourth place in the AL West.

Broadcasting billionaire Tom Hicks, who had bought the Rangers franchise in 1998, was determined to build a World-Series-winning team. So he made a move in 2000 that sent ripples throughout the majors, signing free agent shortstop Alex Rodriguez to a 10-year, $252 million contract—the largest contract in baseball history.

The superstar from Seattle had the numbers to back up such a contract, but he had a lot to live up to in Texas. Many baseball fans were frustrated with what they saw as greedy pro athletes, and baseball experts questioned the precedent such a jaw-dropping contract set. "Our judgment is that Alex will break every record in baseball before he finishes his career," Hicks countered. "And he's a great asset to the community and fans." Indeed, "A-Rod" put his bat where his money was, posting a .318 batting average, 52 home runs, and 135 RBI in his first Texas season. But it wasn't enough; Texas finished the 2001 season 73–89.

CENTER FIELDER · RUSTY GREER

When Rusty Greer came up to the big leagues in 1994, he quickly became a fan favorite. Whether he was diving for a catch or running into the outfield wall to rob an opponent of a home run, Greer gave his all in every inning of every game he played. And he didn't slack off behind the plate either. Greer drove in a game-winning run 17 times and ranks in the Rangers' all-time top five in doubles, triples, walks, runs, total bases, and extra-base hits. In honor of Greer's dedication to the team and the game, the franchise held "Rusty Greer Day" on July 10, 2005.

STATS

Rangers seasons: 1994–2002

Height: 6-0

Weight: 190

- **614 career RBI**
- **519 career walks**
- **258 career doubles**
- **.305 career BA**

RUSTY GREER
CENTER FIELDER

TEXAS
RANGERS

RIGHT FIELDER · **JUAN GONZALEZ**

"Juan Gone" rarely let a hittable pitch go by. The right-handed power hitter signed with the Rangers when he was only 16 years old but didn't become a regular player until he was 22. Within a year, he was leading the league in homers and runs. Gonzalez's bat helped propel the Rangers to three postseason appearances and won him a slew of awards. Three times in his career, Gonzalez hit three homers in one game. And in 1998, he became the second player in history to rack up 100 or more RBI by the midseason All-Star break.

STATS

Rangers seasons: 1989–99, 2002–03

Height: 6-3

Weight: 210

- **434 career HR**

- **1,404 career RBI**

- **2-time AL MVP**

- **3-time All-Star**

JUAN GONZALEZ
RIGHT FIELDER

TEXAS
RANGERS

RUSTY GREER

Throughout a nine-year career, Rusty Greer was loved by fans for his hustle and all-out effort on every play.

THE REAL POSTSEASON

On October 1, 1996, the Rangers had a lot to prove. Two years before, they had been first in the AL West but never played in the postseason because of a strike. This year, their 90–72 record had earned them a postseason showdown with the mighty New York Yankees. The Yanks held the Texas boys at bay in the first inning of Game 1, then followed up by scoring the first run of the game. The next two innings for the Rangers were filled with fly balls and groundouts. Then, in the fourth, Rangers catcher Ivan Rodriguez blooped a single to right field, and Yankees hurler David Cone walked center fielder Rusty Greer, moving "Pudge" to second. With two on and no outs, right fielder Juan Gonzalez stepped to the plate. After a couple of tosses from Cone, "Juan Gone" cranked one out of the park, and the Rangers took the lead. Third baseman Dean Palmer followed that up with another homer in the same inning, giving the Rangers' pitchers some breathing room. New York managed to score only one more run the rest of the way. Although Texas would lose the series, it had won its first postseason game— and against the most successful team of all time.

Before the 2002 season began, Johnny Oates stepped down as manager. His departure seemed to hurt the club, which went 72–90 on the year. After the season, several key players departed as well. Fan favorites Kenny Rogers and Ivan Rodriguez left for other teams, while Rusty Greer retired from the game.

There were a few highlights in 2003, however, that made the year memorable. Rookie first baseman Mark Teixeira came aboard, slamming 26 homers on the season. And thanks to young third baseman Hank Blalock's two-run homer in the All-Star Game, the AL secured home field advantage in the World Series. For a while it looked as if the Rangers would have a shot at representing the AL in the Series. They held on to first place for much of the season before a losing streak in August knocked them out of the running.

In 2004, the name of the Rangers' stadium changed from The Ballpark at Arlington to Ameriquest Field. The team made personnel changes as well, again trading Palmeiro to the Orioles. A-Rod—who, despite his high salary, had not taken Texas to the promised land—was also traded to the Yankees for slugging second baseman Alfonso Soriano. Soriano became the first Rangers player ever to get six hits in nine innings during a 16–15 victory over the Detroit Tigers on

IVAN RODRIGUEZ

After playing for five teams in five seasons, versatile outfielder Gary Matthews found a home in Texas in 2004.

MANAGER · JOHNNY OATES

Johnny Oates was the most successful manager in Rangers history, and his quiet leadership and meticulous organization led the team to its first three postseason appearances. Popular with both fans and players, Oates's greatest skill was his ability to see the potential in his players—and make sure they saw it, too. Prior to managing the Rangers, Oates was a catcher for five different big-league teams and managed the Baltimore Orioles for four seasons. Oates passed away in 2004, and in August 2005, the Rangers honored their most popular skipper by retiring his number 26 uniform.

STATS

Rangers seasons as manager:
   1995–2001

Height: 5-11

Weight: 188

Managerial Record: 797–746

AL West Titles: 1996, 1998, 1999

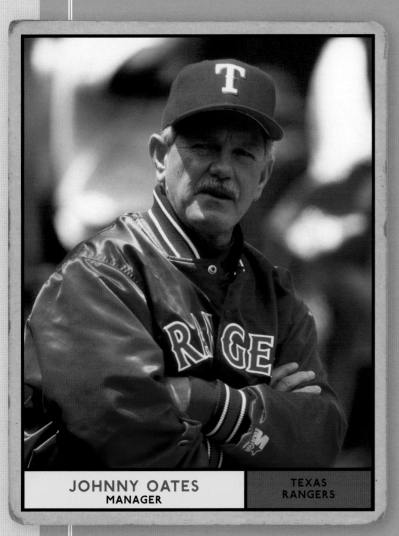

JOHNNY OATES
MANAGER

TEXAS
RANGERS

MARK TEIXEIRA

HIT PARADE

There are days when a team lets its offense do all the work. On such a day, a team can set or tie records simply by sending the right hitter up to the plate. And some games are just what a struggling franchise needs to hit the respectable .500 mark. When the first pitch was tossed in a Seattle Mariners-Texas Rangers matchup on September 18, 2005, nobody realized the significance the game would have in major-league history. However, after nine innings, four Rangers players—David Dellucci, Rod Barajas, Alfonso Soriano, and Mark Teixeira—had all knocked dingers out of the

park. Teixeira awed the crowd with two long balls—one from either side of the plate. The Rangers won the game, 8–6, which placed them squarely at .500. The hit parade gave the team a franchise-record 152 homers at home in one season. It also allowed Texas to set a team record for total homers in a season (260), the third-highest single-season count in major-league history. Barajas's solo homer in the fourth tied another big-league record, giving Texas seven players with 20 or more home runs in one season. All in all, it was a good day for the Rangers.

May 8. But even Soriano's All-Star-caliber performances weren't enough to take the team to the playoffs. The Rangers finished 2004 a much-improved 89–73 but third in the AL West.

The 2005 and 2006 seasons were mediocre ones for the Rangers, who remained in the middle of the AL West pack with 79–83 and 80–82 records. Still, there were signs that better days were ahead. Soriano had left town, but Blalock established himself as one of the game's top third basemen, Teixeira hit 43 homers with 144 RBI in 2005, and shortstop Michael Young won MVP honors in the 2006 All-Star Game. The team also featured an improving pitching rotation led by veteran hurler Kevin Millwood and newly acquired Brandon McCarthy. "The overall expectation is winning," new manager Ron Washington said of his team's outlook before the 2007 season began.

Since migrating to Texas more than 30 years ago, the Rangers have continued to bounce back from adversity with a resilience that the lawmen of the Old West would have admired. And although it took a quarter century for the team to earn its first division title, with such players as Mark Teixeira and Michael Young leading the way, these modern-day Rangers are determined to lasso their first World Series title soon.